The Forgotten Art of Being a Lady

a self-improvement journal
Vol. 2

Guard Your Reputation

The Forgotten Art of Being a Lady

a self-improvement journal Vol.2

Guard Your Reputation

Q

Global Quill Production

Tallahassee, Florida

This is a self-improvement journal to be used for your personal improvement. Use at your own discretion.

This book is published by CreateSpace for: Global Quill Production, LLC Tallahassee, Florida
ISBN-13: 978-0-9979229-1-2
Email to: globalquill@gmail.com

Visit our website at: http://globalquillproduction.webs.com/

Cover design by: Monique Bowden Guice

Edited by: Cynthia M. Portalatin

Graphics by: bigstock.com

Global Quill Production, LLC

Dedication

This is dedicated to all women trying to find their way. Let this book serve as one of the lights along your path.

Consider your reputation as your brand.

Guard it carefully.

TABLE OF CONTENTS

Introduction

Think about a business that you frequent. What sort of reputation does it have? Is it a reputation for being neat and clean? Is it a reputation for giving fast, friendly service? Or does it have the reputation for being dirty and junky with rude, unprofessional associates?

Which business would you rather frequent? Most of us would rather deal with the business that is clean, with great service. That's the reason just about all businesses that advertise on the internet have a comment section. People want to know what they are dealing with. Be it good or bad, the business has developed a reputation. The same is true with people.

Before the internet was invented, word of mouth carried public opinion far and wide. Colorful phrases like "good for nothing," "lazy," "loose," and "low class" stuck to a person like a tattoo on the middle of a person's forehead in flashing neon lights.

For that reason years ago, when young ladies were growing up, they were often asked, "Is that the type of reputation you want to have?" Or they were admonished, "You're going to get a bad reputation." Though a lot of the time these reminders had to do with how a young lady conducted herself with members of the opposite sex, it was easy to forget there were so many other things that went into building one's reputation.

For example, questions indicating character also included: Is she trustworthy or a liar? Is she on time, or is she always late? Is she respectful to her elders? Does she keep her word? Does she produce good, quality work? Will she take responsibility for her actions?

Through the years, reminders about guarding your reputation have been not been openly expressed as much as they once were. Yet, the fact remains – your reputation goes before you. In most cases, a young lady does not have a page on the internet that bares the comments of other people, but somehow word still gets around.

In this journal, we will explore some things that are common but have a large bearing on how we build our reputations. You will be given the opportunity to explore these observations and journal the areas that need improvement along with the steps you can take to make improvements.

Remember, you are your own masterpiece. Color yourself with perfection.

Modesty is not Overrated

A little mystery never hurt anyone.

Look in the mirror. Are your arms bare? What about your chest? Are your breasts barely contained? Do you have to pull your skirt down with every step you take? When your hands are at your side, are they longer than your skirt? Do you show more skin then you cover?

If any of these things happen, it may be time to take pause. Modesty is still supremely important. Your choice of dress "colors" how others perceive you. Your style of dress reflects your personality in many ways, and though it may not completely define you, people will make assumptions about you based on your attire.

We have all heard it said countless times, "I don't care what people think of me." To that I say, "Coward." Coward, because you are not able to face the changes you may need to improve yourself.

Be honest; do you look like a prostitute? Do you look homeless? Do you look like a suburban housewife? A ghetto side chick? An escapee from a mental institute? A business professional? A school teacher? A mother of the church? A nun? A college co-ed? Did any of these labels conjure an image for you? If so, what was your reaction?

You must decide how you want to be seen, how others see and react to you. Decide on the changes needed for that image to be perceived. Include those changes as part of your daily routine.

Find pictures that represent the look you are going for in your style. Gather the needed garments, and include them in your dress for the day. Note the reaction of others to your new look, and journal how you feel.

What Happened?	How I reacted
_____	_____
_____	_____
_____	_____
_____	_____
_____	_____
_____	_____
_____	_____
_____	_____
_____	_____
_____	_____
_____	_____
_____	_____
_____	_____
_____	_____
_____	_____
_____	_____
_____	_____
_____	_____

My Plan of Action

_____
_____
_____
_____
_____
_____

Date:

Find pictures that represent the look you are going for in your style. Gather the needed garments, and include them in your dress for the day. Note the reaction of others to your new look, and journal how you feel.

What Happened?	How I reacted
_____	_____
_____	_____
_____	_____
_____	_____
_____	_____
_____	_____
_____	_____
_____	_____
_____	_____
_____	_____
_____	_____
_____	_____
_____	_____
_____	_____
_____	_____
_____	_____
_____	_____
_____	_____

My Plan of Action

_____
_____
_____
_____
_____
_____

Find pictures that represent the look you are going for in your style. Gather the needed garments, and include them in your dress for the day. Note the reaction of others to your new look, and journal how you feel.

What Happened?	How I reacted

My Plan of Action

Date:

Find pictures that represent the look you are going for in your style. Gather the needed garments, and include them in your dress for the day. Note the reaction of others to your new look, and journal how you feel.

What Happened?	How I reacted

My Plan of Action

_____
_____
_____
_____
_____
_____

Date:

Find pictures that represent the look you are going for in your style. Gather the needed garments, and include them in your dress for the day. Note the reaction of others to your new look, and journal how you feel.

What Happened?	How I reacted
_____	_____
_____	_____
_____	_____
_____	_____
_____	_____
_____	_____
_____	_____
_____	_____
_____	_____
_____	_____
_____	_____
_____	_____
_____	_____
_____	_____
_____	_____
_____	_____
_____	_____
_____	_____

My Plan of Action

_____
_____
_____
_____
_____
_____

Always Respect Others

Part of guarding your reputation is knowing how you treat other people. Are you kind to children? How do you view the homeless? Are you generous to the poor? When you speak with your elders, are you patient? Understanding? Kind?

In a conversation with an elder, do you mind your words, facial expressions and body language? Do you give them courtesy and allow them to speak uninterrupted? When you disagree with what they say or do, do you show them respect by keeping your thoughts to yourself?

Earning the respect of an elder can often be a benefit to you. These are people who can advance your career with just a nod of their heads. When you are found worthy, they can groom you to take their place. They are often asked if they know of someone sharp who might be interested in a job or advancement opportunity. You never know where the opportunity might knock, or who will open the prospective door.

That's true for everyone you meet. You can't see the future and you reputation will go before you no matter where you are headed. Treat everyone you meet with respect and let your reputation speak for you.

Mind your manners.. Speak kindly. Say "Yes, ma'am," or "Yes, sir." Remember, "Thank you" and "Please" are always in order. Be willing to lend a helping hand. Make it a habit.

What Happened?	How I reacted
_____	_____
_____	_____
_____	_____
_____	_____
_____	_____
_____	_____
_____	_____
_____	_____
_____	_____
_____	_____
_____	_____
_____	_____
_____	_____
_____	_____
_____	_____
_____	_____
_____	_____

My Plan of Action

_____
_____
_____
_____
_____
_____

Date:

Mind your manners.. Speak kindly. Say "Yes, ma'am," or "Yes, sir." Remember, "Thank you" and "Please" are always in order. Be willing to lend a helping hand. Make it a habit.

What Happened?	How I reacted
_____	_____
_____	_____
_____	_____
_____	_____
_____	_____
_____	_____
_____	_____
_____	_____
_____	_____
_____	_____
_____	_____
_____	_____
_____	_____
_____	_____
_____	_____
_____	_____
_____	_____
_____	_____
_____	_____

My Plan of Action

_____
_____
_____
_____
_____
_____

Mind your manners.. Speak kindly. Say "Yes, ma'am," or "Yes, sir." Remember, "Thank you" and "Please" are always in order. Be willing to lend a helping hand. Make it a habit.

What Happened?	How I reacted

My Plan of Action

Date:

Mind your manners.. Speak kindly. Say "Yes, ma'am," or "Yes, sir." Remember, "Thank you" and "Please" are always in order. Be willing to lend a helping hand. Make it a habit.

What Happened?	How I reacted

My Plan of Action

Mind your manners.. Speak kindly. Say "Yes, ma'am," or "Yes, sir." Remember, "Thank you" and "Please" are always in order. Be willing to lend a helping hand. Make it a habit.

What Happened?	How I reacted
_____	_____
_____	_____
_____	_____
_____	_____
_____	_____
_____	_____
_____	_____
_____	_____
_____	_____
_____	_____
_____	_____
_____	_____
_____	_____
_____	_____
_____	_____
_____	_____
_____	_____

My Plan of Action

_____

_____

_____

_____

_____

_____

Choose Tactful Honesty

There's a fine line between being honest and being rude. Never confuse the two.

This is an exercise that requires much practice. Being asked to give your honest opinion on a subject does not give you license to open your mouth and let words fly. You must always be considerate of what you are saying.

Choosing to use tact means choosing your words in a way that avoids offense. There is an old adage about sticks and stones breaking bones but words not hurting you. Not true at all. In recent times, we have learned that words spoken to children have the power to corrupt their adulthood.

Words are powerful and have long-reaching and long-lasting effects. The effects of cruel words have been the cause of many deep wounds that have festered unseen for a lifetime in many people.

When you speak to someone, choose your words carefully. Ask yourself, "Are these the words I would like someone to say to me? Would I find these words more hurtful then helpful?" If the answer is yes, find another way to phrase your comments.

What Happened?	How I reacted
_____	_____
_____	_____
_____	_____
_____	_____
_____	_____
_____	_____
_____	_____
_____	_____
_____	_____
_____	_____
_____	_____
_____	_____
_____	_____
_____	_____
_____	_____
_____	_____
_____	_____

My Plan of Action

_____

_____

_____

_____

_____

_____

Date:

When you speak to someone, choose your words carefully. Ask yourself, "Are these the words I would like someone to say to me? Would I find these words more hurtful then helpful?" If the answer is yes, find another way to phrase your comments.

What Happened?	How I reacted
_____	_____
_____	_____
_____	_____
_____	_____
_____	_____
_____	_____
_____	_____
_____	_____
_____	_____
_____	_____
_____	_____
_____	_____
_____	_____
_____	_____
_____	_____
_____	_____

My Plan of Action

_____
_____
_____
_____
_____
_____

When you speak to someone, choose your words carefully. Ask yourself, "Are these the words I would like someone to say to me? Would I find these words more hurtful then helpful?" If the answer is yes, find another way to phrase your comments.

What Happened?	How I reacted
_____	_____
_____	_____
_____	_____
_____	_____
_____	_____
_____	_____
_____	_____
_____	_____
_____	_____
_____	_____
_____	_____
_____	_____
_____	_____
_____	_____
_____	_____
_____	_____

My Plan of Action

_____

_____

_____

_____

_____

_____

Date:

When you speak to someone, choose your words carefully. Ask yourself, "Are these the words I would like someone to say to me? Would I find these words more hurtful then helpful?" If the answer is yes, find another way to phrase your comments.

What Happened?	How I reacted
_____	_____
_____	_____
_____	_____
_____	_____
_____	_____
_____	_____
_____	_____
_____	_____
_____	_____
_____	_____
_____	_____
_____	_____
_____	_____
_____	_____
_____	_____
_____	_____

My Plan of Action

_____
_____
_____
_____
_____
_____

Date:

When you speak to someone, choose your words carefully. Ask yourself, "Are these the words I would like someone to say to me? Would I find these words more hurtful then helpful?" If the answer is yes, find another way to phrase your comments.

What Happened?   How I reacted

_____   _____
_____   _____
_____   _____
_____   _____
_____   _____
_____   _____
_____   _____
_____   _____
_____   _____
_____   _____
_____   _____
_____   _____
_____   _____
_____   _____
_____   _____
_____   _____
_____   _____

My Plan of Action

_____
_____
_____
_____
_____
_____

Be Intelligent Not a Know It All

We live in an information age. Anything we want to know can be found in a variety of places in a variety of forms. Information can be dispersed so fast; facts can be checked while you are speaking.

Most people would agree there is something alluring about intelligent people. A person who has taken the time to learn all he or she can about a subject, or even to become an expert on a topic, deserves our respect. However, it must be remembered that no one likes a "know it all."

When you are knowledgeable in a subject, and you may even be the "go-to person" in an area, you must be careful how you answer questions. Never make anyone who comes to you for information feel little or small, if they are not knowledgeable in your area of expertise. Someone else may be more knowledgeable in another area you know little about. After all, we cannot know everything about everything.

While having a conversation, allow others to express information they know on a subject. Ask questions, and express genuine interest in what they are saying.

What Happened?	How I reacted

My Plan of Action

While having a conversation, allow others to express information they know on a subject. Ask questions, and express genuine interest in what they are saying.

What Happened?	How I reacted
_____	_____
_____	_____
_____	_____
_____	_____
_____	_____
_____	_____
_____	_____
_____	_____
_____	_____
_____	_____
_____	_____
_____	_____
_____	_____
_____	_____
_____	_____
_____	_____

My Plan of Action

_____
_____
_____
_____
_____
_____

While having a conversation, allow others to express information they know on a subject. Ask questions, and express genuine interest in what they are saying.

What Happened?	How I reacted

My Plan of Action

While having a conversation, allow others to express information they know on a subject. Ask questions, and express genuine interest in what they are saying.

What Happened?	How I reacted
_____	_____
_____	_____
_____	_____
_____	_____
_____	_____
_____	_____
_____	_____
_____	_____
_____	_____
_____	_____
_____	_____
_____	_____
_____	_____
_____	_____
_____	_____
_____	_____
_____	_____
_____	_____

My Plan of Action

_____
_____
_____
_____
_____
_____

While having a conversation, allow others to express information they know on a subject. Ask questions, and express genuine interest in what they are saying.

What Happened?	How I reacted

My Plan of Action

Word Selection and Tone of Voice is Everything

The tone of voice you choose is as important as the words you have to say. Is your tone judgmental or accusing? Are you using a rude or condescending tone of voice when you are trying to say something to someone? The tone of voice is something we immediately recognize in others when they are speaking to us. A harsh, loud or angry tone of voice can change the meaning of your words and provoke a negative reaction.. Words can be sharp, but if the tone is soothing, the message is not nearly as painful to hear and the message will still come across.

When someone speaks to us in a tone we don't like, we often say they could have found a better way to say what they said. And though we see this flaw in others, we often don't see it in ourselves. Remember, your tone of voice is just as important as the words you select.

When you want to say something to someone that might be difficult for you to say, or difficult for them to hear, decide beforehand what it is you want to say. It is a good idea to choose words that are the least offensive and stand the chance of causing the least amount of conflict.

Try to remember to think, "If someone was going to say these exact same words to me, what is the least offensive way they could say the words without hurting my feelings? What tone of voice would be least cutting to me?"

Date:

Practice saying unpleasant messages in a tone of voice that would not be offensive to you if you were the one listening. Then choose the best time to tell the person what you have to say in as gentle a voice as possible. Make it your practice to speak in gentle tones.

What Happened?

How I reacted

My Plan of Action

Date:

Practice saying unpleasant messages in a tone of voice that would not be offensive to you if you were the one listening. Then choose the best time to tell the person what you have to say in as gentle a voice as possible. Make it your practice to speak in gentle tones.

What Happened?	How I reacted
_____	_____
_____	_____
_____	_____
_____	_____
_____	_____
_____	_____
_____	_____
_____	_____
_____	_____
_____	_____
_____	_____
_____	_____
_____	_____
_____	_____
_____	_____

My Plan of Action

_____
_____
_____
_____
_____
_____

Date:

Practice saying unpleasant messages in a tone of voice that would not be offensive to you if you were the one listening. Then choose the best time to tell the person what you have to say in as gentle a voice as possible. Make it your practice to speak in gentle tones.

What Happened?	How I reacted
_____	_____
_____	_____
_____	_____
_____	_____
_____	_____
_____	_____
_____	_____
_____	_____
_____	_____
_____	_____
_____	_____
_____	_____
_____	_____
_____	_____
_____	_____
_____	_____
_____	_____
_____	_____

My Plan of Action

_____

_____

_____

_____

_____

Date:

Practice saying unpleasant messages in a tone of voice that would not be offensive to you if you were the one listening. Then choose the best time to tell the person what you have to say in as gentle a voice as possible. Make it your practice to speak in gentle tones.

What Happened?   How I reacted

_____   _____
_____   _____
_____   _____
_____   _____
_____   _____
_____   _____
_____   _____
_____   _____
_____   _____
_____   _____
_____   _____
_____   _____
_____   _____
_____   _____
_____   _____
_____   _____

My Plan of Action

_____
_____
_____
_____
_____

Practice saying unpleasant messages in a tone of voice that would not be offensive to you if you were the one listening. Then choose the best time to tell the person what you have to say in as gentle a voice as possible. Make it your practice to speak in gentle tones.

What Happened?   How I reacted

_____	_____
_____	_____
_____	_____
_____	_____
_____	_____
_____	_____
_____	_____
_____	_____
_____	_____
_____	_____
_____	_____
_____	_____
_____	_____
_____	_____
_____	_____
_____	_____
_____	_____
_____	_____

My Plan of Action

_____

_____

_____

_____

_____

_____

Resist Peer Pressure.

Peer Pressure is something that never seems to go away. It doesn't matter what age you are, there is always someone trying to influence you or persuade you into doing something. Sometimes it's your friends. Sometimes it's co-workers. From time to time, it could be someone in authority. It doesn't matter who they are, people can still put pressure on you. The only thing worse than someone putting pressure on you is when a whole group of people puts pressure on you.

Realize that no matter what is going on, you are the only one responsible for the decision you make. So, take into careful consideration what the group wants you to do and why they want you to do it. Then, ask yourself if you want to do what they are asking you to do. Again, remember you are the one responsible for your decision.

Once you have made your decision to do what you were asked, or not to do what you were asked, tell the group what you have decided. Then do what you have committed to do. By facing the group and telling them your decision, you will develop the reputation of being a direct, straight-forward person thus earning the respect of others.

When someone puts pressure on you to do something, decide if you want to do it or not. Tell them, in clear terms, what you have decided to do, and do it.

What Happened?	How I reacted
_____	_____
_____	_____
_____	_____
_____	_____
_____	_____
_____	_____
_____	_____
_____	_____
_____	_____
_____	_____
_____	_____
_____	_____
_____	_____
_____	_____
_____	_____
_____	_____
_____	_____
_____	_____
_____	_____
_____	_____

My Plan of Action

_____
_____
_____
_____
_____

When someone puts pressure on you to do something, decide if you want to do it or not. Tell them, in clear terms, what you have decided to do, and do it.

What Happened?	How I reacted
_____	_____
_____	_____
_____	_____
_____	_____
_____	_____
_____	_____
_____	_____
_____	_____
_____	_____
_____	_____
_____	_____
_____	_____
_____	_____
_____	_____
_____	_____
_____	_____

My Plan of Action

_____
_____
_____
_____
_____

When someone puts pressure on you to do something, decide if you want to do it or not. Tell them, in clear terms, what you have decided to do, and do it.

What Happened?	How I reacted

My Plan of Action

When someone puts pressure on you to do something, decide if you want to do it or not. Tell them, in clear terms, what you have decided to do, and do it.

What Happened?	How I reacted
_____	_____
_____	_____
_____	_____
_____	_____
_____	_____
_____	_____
_____	_____
_____	_____
_____	_____
_____	_____
_____	_____
_____	_____
_____	_____
_____	_____
_____	_____
_____	_____
_____	_____

My Plan of Action

_____
_____
_____
_____
_____
_____

When someone puts pressure on you to do something, decide if you want to do it or not. Tell them, in clear terms, what you have decided to do, and do it.

What Happened?	How I reacted

My Plan of Action

Don't Take on More Than You Are Capable of Handling

It is very easy to get caught up in the moment. It happens to all of us at one time or the other. When positive energy is flowing all around a group of people, and everyone is offering up suggestion on how to make a situation better, it is only natural to want to do something... to want to do anything. When that happens, you must remember your skills.

Do you have what it takes to complete the job you are trying to accomplish? Have you ever tried to do something of this magnitude before? How did it turn out? Now, it's time to learn from the past. If you could perform the duties you attempted previously, go for it. However, if you have never attempted a project, and you are not sure of your skill set, let me encourage you.

Don't be too shy to admit to the group you want to help that you are not sure of your abilities. Ask if there is someone with more experience that would not mind helping you. If there is not anyone willing to help you, and you still are interested in doing something, tell the group you are willing to try. This could be the perfect time to either improve your skill set or develop a new one. Either way, don't be afraid to try.

Be honest, up front about your skill set, and let everyone know what you can and cannot do. If you still have the opportunity to work on the project, do your very best with the skills you have, and seek to learn new skills. Make sure to give credit to anyone who works with you and has taken the time to help you on your project.

What Happened?	How I reacted
_____	_____
_____	_____
_____	_____
_____	_____
_____	_____
_____	_____
_____	_____
_____	_____
_____	_____
_____	_____
_____	_____
_____	_____
_____	_____
_____	_____
_____	_____

My Plan of Action

_____
_____
_____
_____
_____
_____
_____

Date:

Be honest, up front about your skill set, and let everyone know what you can and cannot do. If you still have the opportunity to work on the project, do your very best with the skills you have, and seek to learn new skills. Make sure to give credit to anyone who works with you and has taken the time to help you on your project.

What Happened?	How I reacted
_____	_____
_____	_____
_____	_____
_____	_____
_____	_____
_____	_____
_____	_____
_____	_____
_____	_____
_____	_____
_____	_____
_____	_____
_____	_____
_____	_____

My Plan of Action

_____

_____

_____

_____

_____

_____

Be honest, up front about your skill set, and let everyone know what you can and cannot do. If you still have the opportunity to work on the project, do your very best with the skills you have, and seek to learn new skills. Make sure to give credit to anyone who works with you and has taken the time to help you on your project.

What Happened?	How I reacted

My Plan of Action

Date:

Be honest, up front about your skill set, and let everyone know what you can and cannot do. If you still have the opportunity to work on the project, do your very best with the skills you have, and seek to learn new skills. Make sure to give credit to anyone who works with you and has taken the time to help you on your project.

What Happened?

How I reacted

My Plan of Action

Be honest, up front about your skill set, and let everyone know what you can and cannot do. If you still have the opportunity to work on the project, do your very best with the skills you have, and seek to learn new skills. Make sure to give credit to anyone who works with you and has taken the time to help you on your project.

What Happened?	How I reacted

My Plan of Action

Make Sound Decisions.

There are usually two kinds of decisions people make: snap decisions and decisions that take time. Each has its merits.

Both require sound judgment on your part. A snap decision is usually made using only the information that is presented at the time the decision is made, with limited facts. Under those circumstances, we make the best decision we can in the limited time we have.

Almost the same can be said for decisions that take time. The main difference in the two types of decision making is time. Time allows us to gather additional facts and consider the possible outcomes.

Whenever possible, take the time to consider the decision you must make. Remember, doing nothing is also a decision.

When faced with making a big decision, go over several scenarios, and study which outcome will work best for you. Then present your decision in a straightforward, logical manner.

What Happened?	How I reacted

My Plan of Action

Date:

When faced with making a big decision, go over several scenarios, and study which outcome will work best for you. Then present your decision in a straightforward, logical manner.

What Happened?	How I reacted
_____	_____
_____	_____
_____	_____
_____	_____
_____	_____
_____	_____
_____	_____
_____	_____
_____	_____
_____	_____
_____	_____
_____	_____
_____	_____
_____	_____
_____	_____
_____	_____
_____	_____
_____	_____

My Plan of Action

_____
_____
_____
_____
_____
_____
_____

When faced with making a big decision, go over several scenarios, and study which outcome will work best for you. Then present your decision in a straightforward, logical manner.

What Happened?	How I reacted
_____	_____
_____	_____
_____	_____
_____	_____
_____	_____
_____	_____
_____	_____
_____	_____
_____	_____
_____	_____
_____	_____
_____	_____
_____	_____
_____	_____
_____	_____
_____	_____
_____	_____
_____	_____

My Plan of Action

_____

_____

_____

_____

_____

When faced with making a big decision, go over several scenarios, and study which outcome will work best for you. Then present your decision in a straightforward, logical manner.

What Happened?	How I reacted
_____	_____
_____	_____
_____	_____
_____	_____
_____	_____
_____	_____
_____	_____
_____	_____
_____	_____
_____	_____
_____	_____
_____	_____
_____	_____
_____	_____
_____	_____
_____	_____
_____	_____

My Plan of Action

_____
_____
_____
_____
_____
_____

When faced with making a big decision, go over several scenarios, and study which outcome will work best for you. Then present your decision in a straightforward, logical manner.

What Happened?	How I reacted
_____	_____
_____	_____
_____	_____
_____	_____
_____	_____
_____	_____
_____	_____
_____	_____
_____	_____
_____	_____
_____	_____
_____	_____
_____	_____
_____	_____
_____	_____
_____	_____
_____	_____
_____	_____

My Plan of Action

_____
_____
_____
_____
_____
_____

Hold Your Head up But do not Look Down Your Nose.

Posture is very important. Holding your head up when you walk demonstrates you are confident in your abilities and who you are as a person. However, there are those who may use their confidence as a weapon to destroy someone else.

To look down your nose is to treat another with disapproval or disrespect, because you feel you are better than they are. It is extremely hard to say what makes one person think or feel superior to another. Sometimes it's money and social class. Sometimes it's education. Sometimes it's neighborhoods. Sometimes it's a combination of things.

To this, I remind you that each person walks a different journey on this earth. Though their path is different from the path you take, they are no less valuable. Skills learned along the way are different. Not better or worse, just different. To disapprove of a person and treat them with disrespect says more about you then it will ever say about them.

Remember to keep your physical posture straight, but be willing to bend in your mental posture and treat all people with the same respect you want to be treated with.

What Happened?	How I reacted

My Plan of Action

_____
_____
_____
_____
_____
_____

Date:

Remember to keep your physical posture straight, but be willing to bend in your mental posture and treat all people with the same respect you want to be treated with.

What Happened?	How I reacted
_____	_____
_____	_____
_____	_____
_____	_____
_____	_____
_____	_____
_____	_____
_____	_____
_____	_____
_____	_____
_____	_____
_____	_____
_____	_____
_____	_____
_____	_____
_____	_____
_____	_____
_____	_____

My Plan of Action

_____
_____
_____
_____
_____
_____

Remember to keep your physical posture straight, but be willing to bend in your mental posture and treat all people with the same respect you want to be treated with.

What Happened?	How I reacted

My Plan of Action

_____

_____

_____

_____

_____

_____

Date:

Remember to keep your physical posture straight, but be willing to bend in your mental posture and treat all people with the same respect you want to be treated with.

What Happened?	How I reacted
_____	_____
_____	_____
_____	_____
_____	_____
_____	_____
_____	_____
_____	_____
_____	_____
_____	_____
_____	_____
_____	_____
_____	_____
_____	_____
_____	_____
_____	_____
_____	_____
_____	_____

My Plan of Action

_____
_____
_____
_____
_____
_____

Date:

Remember to keep your physical posture straight, but be willing to bend in your mental posture and treat all people with the same respect you want to be treated with.

What Happened?	How I reacted

My Plan of Action

Don't be ashamed of having shame

Dictionary.com gives the definition for shame as: the painful feeling arising from the consciousness of something dishonorable, improper, ridiculous, etc., done by oneself or another: disgrace; ignominy: a fact or circumstance bringing disgrace or regret.

I heard a conversation between two young women. One was telling the other when she gets drunk she allows certain things to happen to her. The other girl seemed mortified. To that the first girl said, "Why are you acting like that? Everyone does it."

The first girl proceeded to scold the other girl like she was an errant, disobedient child. By the time the conversation was over, the mortified girl had changed her tune to "I've just haven't had the chance to do anything like that yet. But this is college, a time for experiments."

I have no reason to think the girl ever participated in such an activity. What concerned me was she was willing to go along with the first girl just to get along with her. There was once a time when the activities the first young woman bragged on would have been deemed unacceptable on so many levels. Women who did things like that were deemed scandalous and shunned by others in their community.

These days, we are much more tolerant of the lifestyles of others, regardless of their choices. We no longer express any shame at all. There was once a time when people had shame. A woman who was called a "B" or a "Ho" would have hung her head and covered her face. Now women allow those names as if they are mating calls. Once, falling drunk in public was shameful. Now, it's considered having a good time. Having a baby without being married was shameful. Now, you are just a "baby mama." Not finishing high school was shameful. Now, it just wasn't for you. Having body odor was considered shameful. Now, you are just expressing you own natural scent. Spending time in prison was shameful. Now, it's "family reunion" time. Using vulgar language in public was shameful. Now, it's considered as just having a conversation.

If someone comments on these things, they are considered to be "judgey" or judgmental. And people would rather conform to shameful behavior than to be considered "judgey."

Yet, I'm here to say our society could use a bit more shame. There is nothing wrong with upholding values and principles that not only make you a better person, but also make this

a better society for all.

Date:

Politely refuse to participate in activities you consider are wrong. If pressed, remind yourself and others that you have no desire to participate in something that could bring shame to you or your family, cause you to feel dishonorable or make you feel you are engaging in improper behavior. Remember to maintain you own, personal integrity no matter what others around you are doing.

What Happened?	How I reacted
_____	_____
_____	_____
_____	_____
_____	_____
_____	_____
_____	_____
_____	_____
_____	_____
_____	_____
_____	_____
_____	_____
_____	_____
_____	_____
_____	_____

My Plan of Action

_____
_____
_____
_____
_____

Date:

Politely refuse to participate in activities you consider are wrong. If pressed, remind yourself and others that you have no desire to participate in something that could bring shame to you or your family, cause you to feel dishonorable or make you feel you are engaging in improper behavior. Remember to maintain you own, personal integrity no matter what others around you are doing.

What Happened?

How I reacted

_____ _____
_____ _____
_____ _____
_____ _____
_____ _____
_____ _____
_____ _____
_____ _____
_____ _____
_____ _____
_____ _____
_____ _____
_____ _____
_____ _____
_____ _____
_____ _____
_____ _____
_____ _____

My Plan of Action

_____
_____
_____
_____
_____
_____
_____

Politely refuse to participate in activities you consider are wrong. If pressed, remind yourself and others that you have no desire to participate in something that could bring shame to you or your family, cause you to feel dishonorable or make you feel you are engaging in improper behavior. Remember to maintain you own, personal integrity no matter what others around you are doing.

What Happened?

How I reacted

_____ _____
_____ _____
_____ _____
_____ _____
_____ _____
_____ _____
_____ _____
_____ _____
_____ _____
_____ _____
_____ _____
_____ _____
_____ _____
_____ _____
_____ _____
_____ _____
_____ _____

My Plan of Action

_____
_____
_____
_____
_____
_____
_____

Date:

Politely refuse to participate in activities you consider are wrong. If pressed, remind yourself and others that you have no desire to participate in something that could bring shame to you or your family, cause you to feel dishonorable or make you feel you are engaging in improper behavior. Remember to maintain you own, personal integrity no matter what others around you are doing.

What Happened?	How I reacted
_____	_____
_____	_____
_____	_____
_____	_____
_____	_____
_____	_____
_____	_____
_____	_____
_____	_____
_____	_____
_____	_____
_____	_____
_____	_____
_____	_____
_____	_____
_____	_____

My Plan of Action

_____
_____
_____
_____
_____
_____

Date:

Politely refuse to participate in activities you consider are wrong. If pressed, remind yourself and others that you have no desire to participate in something that could bring shame to you or your family, cause you to feel dishonorable or make you feel you are engaging in improper behavior. Remember to maintain you own, personal integrity no matter what others around you are doing.

What Happened?

How I reacted

My Plan of Action

72

As you make your journey you might discover additional areas you want to improve on.

Use this area to note your progress.

Date:

What Happened?

_____
_____
_____
_____
_____
_____
_____
_____
_____
_____
_____
_____
_____
_____
_____
_____
_____
_____
_____
_____
_____
_____

How I reacted

_____
_____
_____
_____
_____
_____
_____
_____
_____
_____
_____
_____
_____
_____
_____
_____
_____
_____
_____
_____
_____
_____

My Plan of Action

_____
_____
_____
_____
_____
_____

Date:

What Happened?

How I reacted

_____ _____
_____ _____
_____ _____
_____ _____
_____ _____
_____ _____
_____ _____
_____ _____
_____ _____
_____ _____
_____ _____
_____ _____
_____ _____
_____ _____
_____ _____
_____ _____
_____ _____
_____ _____

My Plan of Action

_____
_____
_____
_____
_____
_____

What Happened?

How I reacted

_____   _____
_____   _____
_____   _____
_____   _____
_____   _____
_____   _____
_____   _____
_____   _____
_____   _____
_____   _____
_____   _____
_____   _____
_____   _____
_____   _____
_____   _____
_____   _____
_____   _____
_____   _____

My Plan of Action

_____
_____
_____
_____
_____
_____
_____

Date:

What Happened?

How I reacted

_____   _____
_____   _____
_____   _____
_____   _____
_____   _____
_____   _____
_____   _____
_____   _____
_____   _____
_____   _____
_____   _____
_____   _____
_____   _____
_____   _____
_____   _____
_____   _____
_____   _____
_____   _____
_____   _____
_____   _____

My Plan of Action

_____
_____
_____
_____
_____
_____

What Happened?

How I reacted

My Plan of Action

Date:

What Happened?	How I reacted
_____	_____
_____	_____
_____	_____
_____	_____
_____	_____
_____	_____
_____	_____
_____	_____
_____	_____
_____	_____
_____	_____
_____	_____
_____	_____
_____	_____
_____	_____
_____	_____
_____	_____
_____	_____

My Plan of Action

_____

_____

_____

_____

_____

_____

What Happened?

How I reacted

_____   _____
_____   _____
_____   _____
_____   _____
_____   _____
_____   _____
_____   _____
_____   _____
_____   _____
_____   _____
_____   _____
_____   _____
_____   _____
_____   _____
_____   _____
_____   _____
_____   _____
_____   _____

My Plan of Action

_____
_____
_____
_____
_____
_____

About The Author

Monique Bowden Guice attended Indiana University and Barry University. Presently, she is working on several books. Monique plans to write and publish in several genres.

Her books, The First: a vampire tale, The Forgotten Art of Being a Lady: a self-improvement journal Vol.1, and The Forgotten Art of Being a Lady: a self- improvement journal Vol. 2 Guard Your Reputation are published by Global Quill Production, LLC, where Monique is the founder.

Currently, she lives in Tallahassee, Florida, with her husband. She has one child. Monique is a member of the Tallahassee Authors Network and the Writers Workshop. She would like to thank both groups for their continued support of her writing.

Non-Fiction Titles

The Forgotten Art of Being a Lady Vol. 1

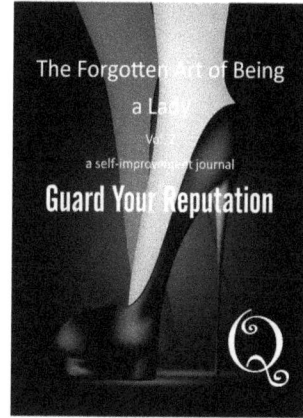

The Forgotten Art of Being a Lady Vol. 2
Guard Your Reputation

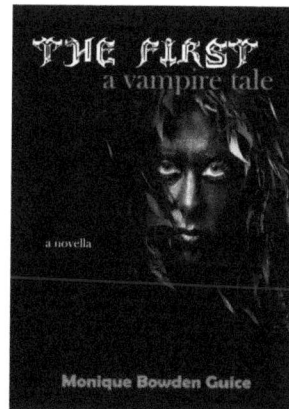

Fiction Titles

The First: a vampire tale

Monique can be reached for reading, speaking engagements and   developmental editing at:

globalquill@gmail.com

Text your questions and info to: (850) 445.0409

Coming Soon

The Forgotten Art of Being a Lady

a self-improvement journal

Vol. 3

The Social Graces

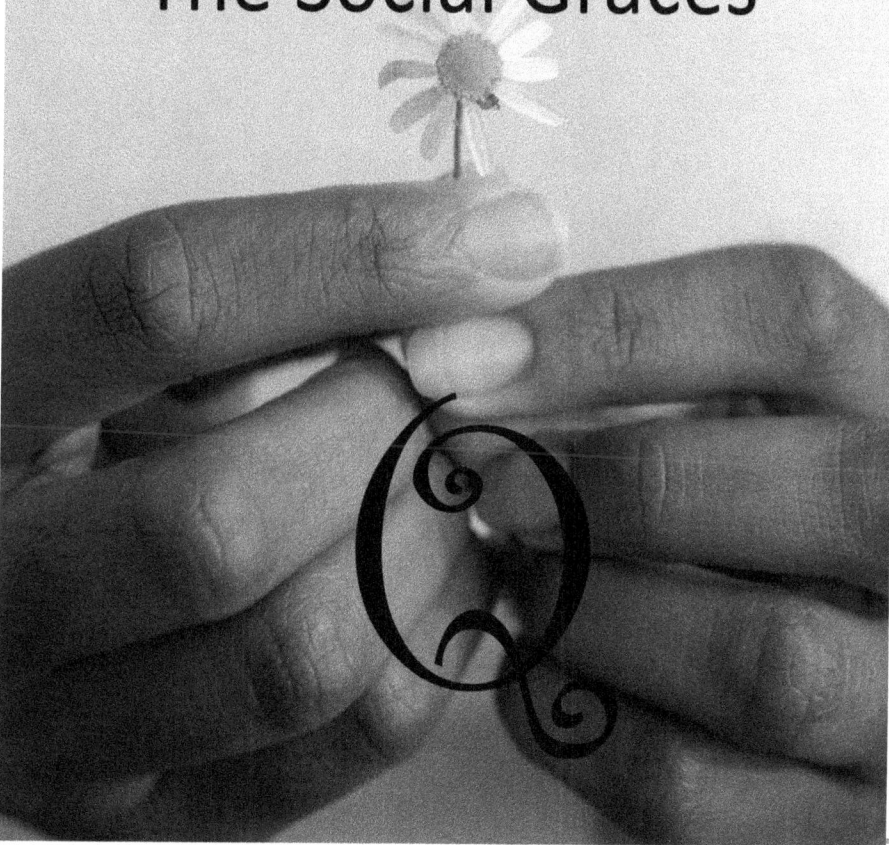

www.ingramcontent.com/pod-product-compliance
Lightning Source LLC
Chambersburg PA
CBHW081635040426
42449CB00014B/3326